Just the Facts

Animal
Welfare

Bel Browning

www.heinemann.co.uk
Visit our website to find out more information about **Heinemann Library** books.

To order:
☎ Phone 44 (0) 1865 888066
🖹 Send a fax to 44 (0) 1865 314091
💻 Visit the Heinemann Bookshop at www.heinemann.co.uk to browse our catalogue and order online.

Produced by Monkey Puzzle Media Ltd, Gissing's Farm, Fressingfield, Suffolk IP21 5SH, UK

First published in Great Britain by Heinemann Library, Halley Court, Jordan Hill, Oxford OX2 8EJ, part of Harcourt Education. Heinemann is a registered trademark of Harcourt Education Ltd.

Editorial: Nick Hunter and Jennifer Tubbs
Series design: Mayer Media
Book design: Jane Hawkins
Production: Viv Hichens

Originated by Dot Gradations Ltd
Printed and bound in Hong Kong, China by South China Printers

ISBN 0 431 16141 0

06 05 04 03 02
10 9 8 7 6 5 4 3 2 1

British Library Cataloguing in Publication Data
Browning, Bel
  Animal welfare. - (Just the Facts)
  1.Animal Welfare - Juvenile literature
  I. Title
  636'.0832

Acknowledgements
The publishers would like to thank the following for permission to reproduce photographs: Associated Press 15 (Suzanne Plunkett), 33 (Keith Weller), 40-41 (Humane Society); Bridgeman Art Library 10-11 (Private Collection); Corbis 8-9 (Paul A Souders), 12-13 (Museum of the City of New York), 21 (Gail Mooney), 34 (Jeremy Horner), 48 (Kevin Fleming); Corbis Stockmarket 4 (Ted Horowitz), 5 (Mug Shots), 49 (Tom Stewart); FLPA 27 (Peter Dean), 43 (Minden Pictures); MPM Images 2-3, 6-7; Nature Picture Library 24-25 (Lynne M Stone); RSPCA Photolibrary 29 (Rex Harper), 30 (Liz Cook), 31, 37 (Ron Kirkby), 39 (Paul Vodden), 46-47 (Alban Donohoe); Popperfoto 44 (Reuters), 45 (Reuters); Still Pictures 14 (Laurent Touzeau), 16-17 (Heine Pedersen), 18 (Daniel Dancer), 19 (Aldo Brando), 20 (Roland Seitre), 22 (Detlef Konner), 23 (Klein/Hubert), 26 (Thomas Raupach), 28 (M & C Denis-Huot), 35 (Harmut Schwarzbach), 38 (Michel Gunther), 51 (J J Alcalay).

Cover photograph reproduced with permission of NHPA.

Every effort has been made to contact copyright holders of any material reproduced in this book. Any omissions will be rectified in subsequent printings if notice is given to the publishers.

Any words appearing in the text in bold, like this, are explained in the Glossary.

Contents

Introduction

Animal welfare is an everyday issue – yet it is one that can provoke strong reactions. Influenced by science, economics and ethics, it considers the treatment that animals receive from humans. The well-being of an animal is determined by factors such as whether it suffers, and if it is healthy. The study of animal welfare must ask questions like:

- What effect do human actions have on animals?
- Should people try to improve animals' lives – and how?
- How can people find out about pain and suffering in animals?

People share this planet with millions of other animal species. Humans are distinguished from these species by complex societies and communication, and the technology they have created. Human intelligence and technology means we now have more power than any other type of animal on earth.

At first, this power was expressed through the hunting of other animals for food. Today, animals are even more important to humans. People eat animals, wear their skins and keep them for work. Drugs and chemicals are tested on them. They are used for sport – such as horse and dog racing, and entertainment – in circuses, for example. They are doted on as pets, and sometimes used as religious symbols.

For centuries now, opinion has been divided over animals. At one extreme are animal rights campaigners, who believe that we should not even keep pets, let alone experiment on or eat animals. At the other end of the scale are those who argue that animals require no consideration at all. Like coal or crops, they are a resource that humans can use to meet their needs, and human welfare comes first.

Many people occupy a middle ground. They may keep pets, yet be vegetarian. They may buy cruelty-free cosmetics, yet enjoy hunting. These viewpoints may even change with circumstance. If a person were starving, they would be more likely to eat meat that they would not normally touch.

Animal welfare has a long history, but is in the news today more than ever before. On average a person eats 1100 animals during their life. RSPCA Australia investigated 55,263 cruelty complaints in 1997–98. The year 2000 saw 2.71 million animals undergo scientific experiments in the UK. Over 13 million unwanted pets are destroyed each year in the USA. This book looks at why animal welfare issues are so important, and how they affect people today.

Boys watch a bear through the glass side of its tank, at a US zoo.

What is animal welfare?

Despite the fact that humans have lived on earth for millions of years, it was only as recently as 1948 that human rights were set down. The Universal Declaration of Human Rights, agreed to by many nations around the world, describes basic rights such as 'the right to life, liberty and security of person.'

If humans deserve rights, do animals? Those who think animals do not point out that humans are very different from other animals. Humans have the ability to reason, build machines and use complex communication systems. People's intellectual and cultural superiority, some argue, means they deserve different treatment from animals. Human illness, starvation and suffering should be reduced, whatever the consequences for animals.

Other people want animals to have rights, saying that they have many similar needs and feelings even if they are less intelligent. Those who support animal welfare believe that whether we give animals rights or not, we still have a responsibility to look after them.

What about welfare?

Welfare is the state of well-being in which basic needs are met and suffering is minimized. Animal welfare is concerned with the suffering of individual animals and ways to improve their well-being – not just the threat to a species. People can recognize issues affecting their own welfare – such as hunger and thirst – but in animals, hunger behaviour, for example, may be hard to distinguish from thirst or distress.

In fact, in recent years it has been proven that animals have specific needs. If these needs are not met, then welfare may be compromised. In response to this discovery, the Farm Animal Welfare Council, an internationally recognized organization that advises UK government developed the Five Freedoms as standards for farm animals:

- Freedom from hunger and thirst
- Freedom from discomfort
- Freedom from pain, injury and disease
- Freedom from fear and distress
- Freedom to express normal behaviour.

These Freedoms now form the basis of policies and standards for many animal welfare organizations. In addition the Freedoms are slowly finding their way into legislation around the world.

"It matters not to the animal how we feel but what we do."

(John Webster in *Animal Welfare*, published 1994)

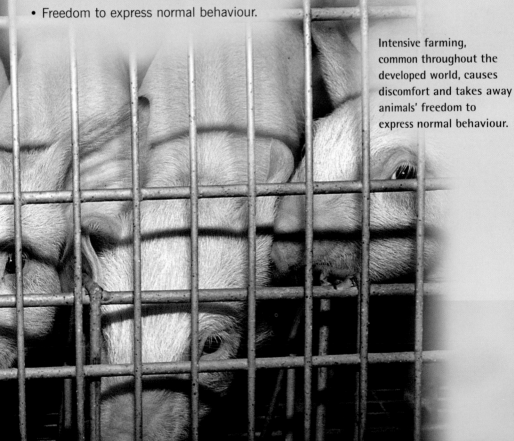

Intensive farming, common throughout the developed world, causes discomfort and takes away animals' freedom to express normal behaviour.

Pain and suffering

One of the problems with discussions about animal welfare is that the animals themselves cannot tell us how they feel. Instead people must study them to find out answers to questions such as: do animals feel pain? Do animals suffer? Is suffering cruelty?

Physical pain

Physical pain is the body's way of protecting itself. When you touch something hot you feel pain and move away, which limits the damage done. In order to feel pain, an organism needs a highly developed nervous system. Nerve endings detect sensations like pain or temperature and tell the brain. The brain's pain centre dulls pain by causing the release of **hormone** painkillers such as **endorphins** and **cortisones**.

Mammals, fish and birds all have pain control centres in their brains. All vertebrate animals produce pain-controlling substances like endorphins too. In fact, even earthworms have been found to make endorphins.

Being separated from the rest of the flock is highly stressful for sheep.

Mental and emotional pain

It may be easy to spot poor physical health, but we cannot read an animal's mind to find out what it is feeling. However, evidence does suggest that animals experience mental pain and stress. In one experiment researchers measured hormone levels in sheep while they were being loaded into a truck, or put through a sheep dip, or being chased by a dog. Levels of cortisone-type hormones, used as painkillers by the body, rose in all these situations. This indicates a high level of stress and pain in the experimental subjects. The worst affected were those sheep separated from the flock. It appears that to a sheep, a solo dip is much more stressful than being taken to the slaughterhouse with the rest of the flock.

Suffering and sentience

Pain causes suffering. Since we know that mammals, birds and fish at least can feel pain, we might conclude that they suffer too. The capacity to suffer by feeling pain, injury and discomfort is described as **sentience**. Animals that are judged at present to be non-**sentient** include insects, spiders and shellfish. New Zealand is one of the few places that recognizes crabs and lobsters as sentient and has laws to protect them. The sentience of an animal affects how we treat it in the law and in practice. Causing pain and suffering is an act of cruelty both ethically and legally.

One danger of exploring animal needs is that we may fall into the trap of **anthropomorphism** – assuming animals think and feel as we do. The sheer number of cartoons with talking, thinking animals shows how common anthropomorphism is in our everyday lives. It is incorrect to assume animals have our needs or emotions.

The history of animals and people

The story of people on earth is one of competition between humans and the rest of the animal kingdom. The first humans were hunter-gatherers. They collected seeds and fruits and caught animals for food and clothing. Cave paintings show brutal and dangerous kills – as harmful to people as to their prey. The contest could be almost equal for both combatants.

Around 12,000 years ago people first began to practise agriculture. Tribes settled on plots of land where they grew crops and kept animals. These people began the slow process of **domesticating** and taming animals such as cattle. Domestication offers the advantages of food and safety to animals. These animals had to be kept in conditions good enough to allow them to do their work or be slaughtered for food at the required time. Humans gained a guaranteed supply of working animals and food that could be harvested on demand.

Super animals

Once animals were under human control, people could start to improve their quality. Choosing to mate the best

animals together, farmers could breed ever better offspring. Most domestic animals today are much larger than their wild relatives. They produce more milk, or are easier to herd, or give birth to more young. These 'super animals' now need us as much as we need them. The Belgian Blue cow, for example, bred to be 'double muscled' for extra meat, cannot give birth without human intervention: a Belgian Blue calf is usually born by **Caesarean section** because it is already too big for natural birth.

'Super animals' were bred and proudly displayed in the 18th and 19th centuries. This Gloucester Old Spot pig was painted in Staffordshire, UK.

Ancient Egypt

Throughout human history people have tamed and changed animals. At times, they have also shown them great respect. Ancient Egyptians are known to have worshipped animal gods like the jackal Anubis. They are also famed for their love of cats. In a cemetery near Cairo 180,000 **embalmed** cats were recently discovered. Only rich people could afford embalming, so cats must have been highly prized.

Blood sport

In contrast to the Egyptians, ancient Romans mutilated and killed thousands of animals in lavish public festivals. When the Colosseum was opened 5000 animals were killed in just one day. Similar rituals and festivals continue to be popular throughout the world today in the form of bullfighting, and cock and dog fights.

At the same time as enjoying these bloodthirsty sports, the Romans built up strong relationships with other animals. Dogs were tamed for protection and to help with hunting. Donkeys and oxen were used for work, cows, goats and sheep to provide milk and meat, and horses for travel.

Seeds of change

As animals began to feature in the domestic lives of humans, so the relationship between the two started to change. Having more contact with tamed animals allowed people insight into animal behaviour and instincts. For some, there might be profit to be made from this behaviour – perhaps the retrieving skills of a dog. In others, experiences with a pet might mean they had a great sympathy for animals.

Significant campaigns for animal welfare began just over 200 years ago. Before this time many religions hinted at some obligation to animals out of respect for the Creator, but many people saw animals as little more than machines. Early animal welfare campaigners came from the wealthier parts of society: the rich came into contact with animals through riding or as pets, and had the time and influence to become involved in making animal welfare laws.

The law now protects animals in many countries. Although animals may be offered a greater consideration, sympathy is not unanimous (agreed by all). When **bull baiting** was banned in the UK in 1835, not everyone approved. Just years earlier in 1827, the prime minister, George Canning, had commented on bull baiting that 'the amusement inspired courage and produced a nobleness of sentiment and elevation of mind'. Much of the general public agreed with Canning, since this sport gave entertainment in both town and country. These opinions were overridden by people who asserted that animals were suffering and decided to act in their defence.

Scientific knowledge played some part in fostering sympathy for animals.

Scientific research and observations gave a better understanding of animals, and this knowledge was passed on to the general public. With the growth of newspapers and cheap books, more people became aware of animal issues.

Another factor was the advance of philosophy and human rights. The abolition of slavery in the British Empire in 1834 sparked consideration of animals and their rights too. As philosophers and intellectuals began to attribute **sentience** to some animals, campaigners began to spread the idea that animals deserved consideration.

As interest in animal welfare began to grow, laws were passed to protect animals. Fostered by this new attitude, the first welfare society, the Society for the Prevention of Cruelty to Animals was formed in the UK, in 1824. Today known as the Royal Society for the Prevention of Cruelty to Animals, it is the oldest animal protection organization in the world.

This painting shows typical American country life for the wealthy in the 19th century, when concern for animal welfare began to grow.

Growth and progress

In recent centuries the global human population has increased rapidly. In 1600 the world's population was an estimated 3.5 million people; today it has grown to roughly 6 thousand million. This population explosion has had an effect on humans and the types of life they lead, as well as on animals.

A direct by-product of the population increase has been the loss of **habitat** for animals. In the developed countries of the North and West, more land must be farmed ever more intensively to support these billions of people. Further land must be developed for housing, roads and industry. Where people have congregated in cities the natural world has had to accommodate rubbish tips, traffic fumes and other pollution.

To afford to eat, and gain a good quality of life, people need jobs. Advancing technology has meant that the majority of new employment is industrial and city based. Few people in cities are able to farm their own food. With basic needs such as food at stake, **intensive farms** have apparently become a necessity. Globally around 43.5 thousand million animals are farmed for food (such as meat and milk) each year.

Foxes often scavenge household waste.

The result of this progress is that humans have an enormous impact on, and influence over, animals' lives. This has prompted people to organize themselves into animal welfare groups. Today there are over 6000 animal welfare organizations around the world.

Some have an interest in all aspects of animal welfare, for example the national SPCA and RSPCA organizations, whilst in contrast, the Anti-Dog-Meat Movement has a specific goal: to end the breeding, sale and consumption of dogs.

Origins of some of the first national animal protection organizations

Country	1st regional organization	National organization	Name of organization
Australia	4th July 1871	1981	RSPCA Australia
New Zealand	1882	1933	Royal New Zealand RSPCA
Scotland	1839	1990s	Scottish SPCA
England and Wales	1824	1824	RSPCA
USA	1866	1866	American SPCA
World	1953	1981	World Society for the Protection of Animals

A global viewpoint

As human science and technology develop and populations grow, so the demands on animals increase. We need to feed and house billions of people, some of whom do not have enough to eat. Doing this while making sure that all animals live in ideal circumstances is impossible. Animal and human welfare are often in opposition. Sometimes, however, a single global cause unites people from a wide variety of backgrounds to fight for animal welfare.

Whaling

In 1986 the International Whaling Commission placed a **moratorium** or ban on commercial whale hunting for food and scientific research. This was brought about by continued pressure from conservation and animal welfare organizations around the world.

Whaling in Iceland.

Falling whale numbers and the inhumane killing techniques used had shocked members of these organizations and the general public.

Most countries stuck to this ban, but 20,000 whales have since been killed for food, cosmetics and scientific reasons. Technology has made whale products such as oil and whalebone unnecessary, but they are still desirable as luxury goods, fuelling the continued harpooning of **endangered** whale species.

Elephant attack

Another instance of a clash between people and animals comes from India. Population growth has forced farmers to convert more and more forest into agricultural land. This forest was the home of elephants, which have now taken to raiding farms and attacking people. In July and August 2001, twenty elephants were deliberately poisoned in Sonitpur, near Nameri National Park. In September, eleven more elephants died a similar death. Local people trying to protect their crops from damage were almost certainly responsible.

Media watch

Daily papers often seize upon animal stories with delight, knowing how popular they will be. In the summer of 2001, suicide bombers were attacking Jerusalem and the trials of suspects of the US embassy bombings in Nairobi, Tanzania and Kenya were under way. The media, however, homed in on a different story. In Washington State a moose was spotted cooling off in a swimming pool. It made headline news around the world.

Wildlife

Wildlife and humans are often in opposition. Humans affect the lives of wild animals in many important ways.

Through activities such as logging, building, farming and polluting humans destroy animal **habitats**. Many of the animals on our planet have become specialized to suit a particular habitat. If this disappears because of human activity – draining wetlands or cutting down woodlands for example – they cannot survive.

Killing animals for food and sport by hunting and **snaring** is common practice across the globe – Americans, for example, hunt over 200 million animals each year. Some of these animals are for food, some to control populations and others for recreation. Death is often quick and efficient – but not always. An animal that is injured in a hunt but gets away may take weeks to die. Snares are not selective at all and can trap or harm any animal that gets caught in them. Supporters of hunting with dogs argue that it offers the best way to control animal numbers, but the **quarry** may be chased to exhaustion for many kilometres before capture and death.

The rubbish – wrappers and bags and cans – that people discard can be deadly to wild animals. They may get trapped inside metal cans, or choke on plastic bags. In 1998 a dead whale was washed ashore on the Spanish coast. Its stomach contained a deadly meal of over 20 kilograms of plastic bags and bottles.

Thousands of wild animals get killed and injured on roads each year. Frog crossings and other schemes to put tunnels under roads are very good at helping with this problem.

Animals, particularly marine fish and **corals**, are often taken from the wild and left to dry and die in the sun to be sold as souvenirs. The shells, starfish and sea horses sold in holiday resorts are all harvested from the sea.

Of course, wild animals do not only suffer from the effects of human activity. In the wild, their needs are often not met. Wild animals suffer injury and disease and may lack food and shelter. Their welfare is not guaranteed in nature, and many die relatively young as a result.

Conch fishing in Colombia: conchs are popular tourist souvenirs. Native people can make money easily by plucking them from the sea and selling them.

Deforestation, Oregon, USA. Deforestation causes loss of habitat for many species.

Zoo life

Zoos and **aquariums** have existed for around 4500 years. The first collections of animals were made by the rich and famous out of curiosity, to gain scientific knowledge of behaviour, and as a reflection of their success. Today, zoos are businesses and the 10,000 zoos around the world house between 2 and 5 million animals.

Zoos are seen as important for the preservation of rare species, breeding rare animals for re-introduction into the wild. Zoos are also educational, offering people the chance to observe captive animal behaviour – and this can often be entertaining. In addition, animals have an easy life, not having to hunt for food and shelter.

Zoos do face criticism. In 1994 a survey revealed that only 16 out of 145 re-introduction programmes had

been successful, suggesting that their conservation role needs to be improved. Zoos have a poor conservation record, because in reality not many of them have an active conservation role, preferring to keep more common, easy to care for species. Animals who are in captivity do not always behave in a natural way. They may resort to violence or self-mutilation to relieve boredom. Such troublesome animals may be **put down**; so may the crowd-pulling baby animals when they grow into adults that are harder to manage.

Zoos provoke strong opinions both for and against. Even their supporters recognize that thousands of zoos, especially in poor or war-torn countries, cause suffering. But sometimes zoos have played a useful role in keeping an **endangered** species going, as well as educating people about animals.

In many existing zoos, conditions could be made better. Welfare campaigners say this makes sense not just for the animals but for visitors too, who will see animals leading more normal and healthy lives.

Zoo improvements

Today many zoos are getting to grips with the physical and mental needs of their charges. In a barren enclosure an animal will often resort to **stereotypies** – repeating movements like pacing, or foot chewing, which continues even when the wound bleeds. This is bad for the visitors and the animals.

Stereotypies indicate frustration and stress. The animal is trying to calm itself through repeated behaviour. Environmental enrichment can help stop stereotypies:

- Glasgow Zoo reduces pacing among ocelots by increasing feeding from one to four times a day. Keepers hide chopped meat in a woodpile so the cats spend the day hunting for their food.

- Austin Zoo in Texas hides capuchin monkey treats inside Chinese take-out boxes. The challenge of finding the treats allows the monkeys to use their natural skills and reduces their levels of boredom.

- At Copenhagen Zoo the bears are kept sweet with a honey machine. Honey is pumped into artificial trees at random times of the day. Hearing this, the bears climb the trees and begin the slow and sticky job of collecting the honey.

Farm animals

In the developed world farmers are the only people who live alongside the animals they farm and eat. Many consumers eat and wear animal products with little idea of how the animals lived. Many people still imagine farms to be places with cattle in fields, pigs in pens and chickens scratching in the dirt. The reality can be dramatically different.

Hi-tech farms

Intensive farming systems scarcely resemble traditional farms at all. From the outside these modern farms are neat and tidy rows of long, low buildings. Feeding and cleaning are mechanized. The only signs of life are the trucks that pull into the yards to load up for the slaughterhouse or to deliver feed.

These 'factory' farms have their roots in the last century. Farming had to become more efficient and occupy less space to supply the expanding cities and their desire for fast and cheap food. The USA increased production levels after the First World War when surplus food could be sold at profit to a hungry Europe. After the Second World War, Europeans were tired of food rationing; they wanted meat, and plenty of it. Helped by government funding, the intensive farm was born. Once animal medicines were created to stop disease spreading in the cramped conditions, they became a runaway success.

Farm animals are kept in cages or pens in barns – or even high-rise blocks whose slatted floors allow waste to drop right through. Being inside, animals are easily fed, watered and given medication. Light levels are constant – in the case of laying hens this encourages egg production – or low, to prevent fighting.

For cheap transportation to the slaughterhouse, animals are usually crowded together. Those that fall may be injured or crushed. The open, slatted trucks give little protection against heat or cold – a shock for animals from temperature-controlled near-darkness. Many countries have regulations requiring rest and feeding stops, but these are not always respected. On long journeys mortality rates are high – over 100,000 Australian sheep die each year on the trip to the Middle East, for example, where demand for lamb is high.

Once they reach the slaughterhouse, cows, sheep and pigs are stunned using an electric shock, or a **captive bolt** to the brain. Occasionally this does not work, so some animals are still conscious when they are killed. Cows and pigs are usually killed by having their throats slit.

Animals have been shown to suffer in the very conditions that ensure efficient and cheap production. Modern chickens bred for speedy growth are ready to be eaten at 41 days old. Such speedy growth means intensive animals often have heart and leg defects that can lame or kill them. But these chickens, like other intensively farmed animals, do meet consumer desire for cheap and readily available meat.

ɛɛThese intensively raised animals have no constitution, you know. Sometimes they just seem to get heart failure because of the strain imposed by terrific growth rates. And often their legs or backs seem to give out: they grow so fast that their bone structure cannot keep up.ɟɟ

(Chris Turton, chicken farmer, UK.)

Free range farms

Towards the end of the 20th century, people began to take a greater interest in how their food was produced. Today we can choose to eat meat and other produce from animals raised on non-**intensive** and **free range** farms.

Intensive egg production

In many factory farms laying hens are reared five to a cage, with 450 cm^2 space for each bird. Sheds may hold up to 60,000 birds, whose eggs are collected from the cages by conveyor belt. This is a very economic egg production system, but does have some problems. Hens frequently fight with their cage-mates and pluck out their own feathers to relieve stress. Lack of exercise means brittle bones are common and many die at an early age. Traditional breeds of hen, like their jungle-dwelling ancestors, can be aggressive, so new breeds have been developed with a calmer temperament. Various alternatives to factory farms have developed over the last twenty years.

Perchery systems

Percheries are large barns where hens have bare floor areas with an upper limit of 25 birds per square metre. In addition, each bird has at least 15 cm^2 of perching space.

Deep litter systems

Deep litter birds are also confined to the barn. There is usually a maximum of seven birds per square metre, and a third of the barn floor is covered with litter (bedding). The litter allows the birds to scratch around for food and carry bedding to their nests. Another addition is the presence of an area specifically for the collection of droppings.

Semi-intensive systems

Hens have continuous daytime access to an outside area. On the inside, the barn has the same conditions as perchery or deep litter systems.

The outside compound must have vegetation to allow the chickens to scratch and dust bathe, and overall, birds have at least 2.5 m^2 of space each.

Free range systems

Similar to semi-intensive systems, free-range farms offer the hens continuous daytime access to vegetation outside, and an inside barn. One difference is that each bird now has at least 10 m^2 to move, flap, scratch and bathe in. Hens can choose to be in or outside, and have bedding to explore and nest in.

For the producer and consumer, battery hens produce the cheapest eggs. The labour, land and foodstuffs costs of mass production are lower and this is passed on to the consumer. Barn systems offer more space per hen than batteries, and free range even more. Since active hens eat more, land is expensive, and more people are needed to care for these free ranging birds, the cost to the farmer is higher. In the supermarket, this cost is reflected in the price. Free-range eggs are more expensive for the shopper.

The pig

After 12,000 years of **domestication** pigs still have 'wild boar' traits. Intelligent and inquisitive animals, they root with their snouts for food – bulbs and worms, fruit, seeds and leaves. Life on many farms, especially **intensive farms**, is nothing like this.

Factory farm pigs

Breeding **sows** are confined in small stalls whilst they produce piglets for meat. One popular sow system is the stall and tether system – now banned in some countries. The stall stops the sow turning around or taking more than two steps in any direction during her four-month pregnancy. Originally these stalls were designed to stop sows fighting and make feeding and cleaning easier.

Before farrowing (giving birth) many sows are loaded into farrowing crates. Smaller even than a stall and tether, the sow may only stand up or lie down. She can only move slowly so her piglets have time to escape into the creep (a separate penned area) as she lies down. Once she is down, they can come back through the bars between the creep and the pen and suckle.

Intensively farmed pigs suffer from overcrowding and unnatural conditions.

A sow will have around ten to twelve piglets. At three weeks the piglets are taken for fattening. For the first six weeks this may be in a metal pen. Next, they go to the fattening house, often in bare pens with no bedding. Here they are kept calm by being kept in near darkness with up to 30 others.

Profitable pigs

One of the great things about this system is the quick turnaround of animals. The pigs can be sent to slaughter sooner than if they were raised in a more natural environment. The pigs are also much cheaper to rear using factory methods. Raising the temperature in the shed makes the pigs need less food. Antibiotics in the pig food prevent illness. Also all this requires just one person to manage the process.

Intensive farms have drawbacks. A pregnant sow in the wild builds a large nest for her babies. In a factory farm she becomes agitated and frustrated. Naturally, piglets drink milk up to about three months old. **Weaned** at three weeks on the farm they suffer from the sudden change in food, and the lack of warmth. They are also more likely to fight with other piglets.

Pig fighting, like zoo **stereotypies**, can be stopped. The addition of simple toys like a ball or bale of straw can greatly reduce such behaviour as tail biting. But where economic interest is the driving force, this extra cost may not even be a consideration since it would have to be passed on to the consumer. Where more animal-friendly systems have been introduced in pig farming, meat prices are considerably higher.

Pigs living in a free range system have a more natural lifestyle. They live outside with warm shelters and mud baths, and can move around and root as in the wild.

Companion animals

People keep **domestic** animals for companionship as well as for food. Pets are not bred for meat or milk, but for obedience and friendliness. They are not needed for food, but are kept as a luxury.

Pet life

In the wild, most **sentient** animals grow up in a family. Peers and parents teach skills such as hunting. Adults are usually independent and may view others as competition for food, a companion or a mate.

The lifestyle of a pet-shop pet is totally different. In its most extreme form, pets such as puppies are reared in hundreds in **intensive**-style farms. On these factory farms, puppies are cheap to produce and **weaned** for sale before eight weeks. The mother is re-mated straight away. Puppy farm puppies grow up out of human contact and are shy of people, making them easily trained.

A pet may have little contact with others of its species, and it may never be allowed to mate or breed. This is a very unnatural life, although that in itself may not be a problem. The crucial questions are: can an animal adapt to these circumstances without suffering? Is it our concern if it does suffer?

A wild dog family in Tanzania. These dogs have the freedom of a natural life, but are exposed to the dangers of the wild.

Causes of suffering

We do not know if animals 'enjoy' their everyday lives as pets, but they often seem content. Most pet owners love and care for their pets, giving them toys, food and exercise. Where cruelty takes place, it can be caused by: ignorance – lack of knowledge; neglect – lack of care; or outright cruelty – where suffering is caused by actively inflicted pain.

Animals that are unwanted or abandoned often end up at shelters. Although some can be re-homed, many have to be killed. The USA alone destroys 13 million pets a year. A shelter worker describes the difficulty of this situation: 'There's a terrible paradox in what you will have to do – you will want to care for the animals but you will have to kill some of them.'

"Animals are such agreeable friends – they ask no questions, they pass no criticisms."

(George Eliot, author (1819–1880))

"Many pet animals enjoy a ... higher standard of physical welfare than many children and ... some horses retire into better care than that afforded to some old people."

(James Dewar, *The Rape of Noah's Ark*, 1969)

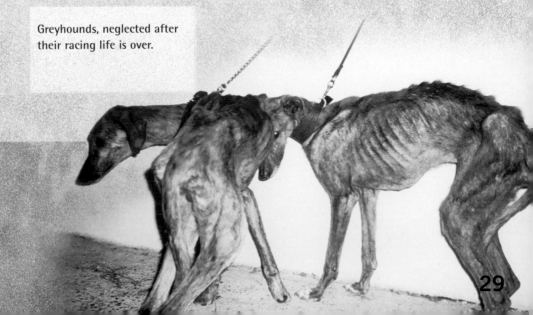

Greyhounds, neglected after their racing life is over.

Research animals

Animals have been used in scientific investigations for centuries. In the 1600s William Harvey studied the circulation of blood by experiments on both people and animals. In the 1800s Louis Pasteur found how to prevent chicken **cholera** through experiments infecting chickens with cholera bacteria. Since this time we have learned valuable scientific information from animal experimentation – sometimes known as **vivisection** – and continue to learn from over 100 million animals used around the world each year.

Why vivisection?

Vivisection has many purposes. Many countries have laws that require new chemicals to be safety-tested on animals before humans can use them. This testing includes new medicines, cosmetics and toiletries, which are tested internally and on the skin. Pioneering new surgical techniques and new vehicles and weapons are tested with animals standing in for people. Other research may be simply biological explorations of how the body works.

Learning from animal experiments can bring new possibilities for people too. Animal **cloning** technology is forecast to lead on to work on humans. Monkeys are in high demand for AIDS research and new therapies are constantly entering the market. Humans benefit from vivisection, in knowledge, health and financially.

Beagles are used for research into the effects of smoking.

What are the alternatives?

Animal experimentation is only one of many techniques used to gain scientific knowledge. There are now several alternatives available.

Humans are the most reliable experimental subjects. For decades beagles have been made to chain smoke so that scientists could investigate how smoking might affect people. More recently the large number of human smokers has been recognized as an equally valuable source of information, but animal tests continue.

Another way to study the effect of drugs and vaccines is through the use of human tissue. Only a small sample of tissue is needed, as it can be grown in a dish and used for testing. Sharing similar cell structure and even some **DNA** with humans, microbes such as yeast and bacteria can also yield realistic drug and vaccine test results. As technology improves, our best test results may soon be at hand. Computer programs such as Cybermouse, which models how a real mouse would respond to tests, can be used in research. Realistic dummies can replace animals in crash tests for vehicles, and weapons tests.

In many countries, scientific research is tightly controlled and monitored by the government. Most experiments must be approved by specially selected panels.

Laboratory rat, bred for experimentation.

Genetic engineering

Genetic engineering is a technique that can be used to manipulate **genes** and produce animals that have improved qualities such as milk yield. It is distantly related to **selective breeding** which has been used for centuries to give us the variety of pet and farm animals existing today. In the UK, 582,000 animals were used for genetic engineering experiments in the year 2000 (Home Office figures).

New and improved

In every living cell of an animal or plant we can find **DNA**. This DNA contains all the information the organism needs to build and maintain the body. A length of the DNA that controls a specific characteristic – such as eye colour – is called a gene.

Genetic engineering aims to change the genetic make up of an organism by altering or moving its existing genes. Animals that have been altered in this way are called **transgenic** animals. Currently, in the early stages of this technology, around 100 animals are involved in the production of every three successful transgenic animals. This allows for transgenic animals that die young from deformity and those not born with the required traits.

Genetic engineering can give us a great deal of new knowledge and practical improvements to animals. We can discover:

- What specific genes do
- How to increase production of meat and milk
- Ways to create disease resistance
- Ways to create animals with diseases, for drug tests
- How to alter animals so we can use them as organ donors.

However, there are some drawbacks. Animals suffer from the experiments and from the conditions they live in. Many tests require sterile conditions and to meet these, animals are separated at birth and live in cages without bedding or company. Animals are bred with deformities and must live under observation, some unable to move or see. Dolly the Sheep, famous for being an identical **cloned** copy of another adult sheep, has developed a painful form of arthritis at a surprisingly early age. Despite the pain she is in, Dolly will not be treated so that scientists can learn more about her sudden disability.

❝The alleviation of human suffering justifies the sacrifice of lower animals.❞

(Robert J White, in *A Defense of Vivisection*,1976)

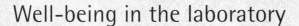

Well-being in the laboratory

Many laboratory animals experience pain and suffering, not just from the experiments they are involved in, but also from the housing conditions. Many are kept in tiny cages with no companions. Self-mutilation is common. In the last few years, though, some researchers have begun to change the environments of research animals.

A type of mouse engineered to have **neurological** problems has trouble walking. This disability allows scientists to study similar human diseases. This mouse, however, gets cold as it cannot make a nest, or reach the food hopper. After intervention by a welfare organization, the laboratory technicians put the food nearer to the mouse and added healthy mice that built a nest for them all.

Genetically altered mouse, shown with a normal mouse. Researchers have genetically engineered mice to grow huge muscles. This may lead to the development of treatments for muscular dystrophy and other muscle-wasting disorders.

Animal welfare: opinions

Opinions are divided when it comes to animal welfare. Some people believe humans have priority over animals, due to superior intelligence and ability, and that animal welfare is not even a consideration. To others all life forms should have equal status and rights. Some issues, such as hunting or experimentation, inspire extreme views both for and against. There is no simple agreement on right and wrong, but a great many perspectives.

Religious viewpoints

Different religious writings portray animals in different ways. In the Jewish-Christian tradition humans have the upper hand:
'Then God said "Let us make man in our image, after our likeness and let them have dominion over the fish of the sea and over the birds of the air, and over the cattle, and over all the earth and over every creeping thing that creeps on the earth."'

(The Bible)

Hinduism has a very different approach to the natural world:
'One should treat animals such as deer, camels, asses, monkeys, mice, snakes, birds and flies exactly like one's own son. How little difference there is between children and these innocent animals.'

(Srimad Bhagavatam)

Hindus honour the cow as the symbol of creation, Mother Earth. White cows wander freely in India.

In Islam the following opinion is expressed:

> 'Doing good to beasts is like the doing of good to human beings, a deed of charity; while cruelty to animals is forbidden, just like cruelty to human beings.'
>
> (Mishkat al Masabidh)

Welfare and rights

Animal welfarists accept that humans have a big impact on animals' lives. They believe that humans have a responsibility for the well-being of animals – to avoid making them suffer, or if this cannot be done, minimizing the suffering inflicted.

Animal rights supporters go further than the welfarists. They believe that animals have the right to be treated with respect and without **exploitation**. This means no animal farming, sport or research. While some work peacefully using education and campaigning to achieve this, others use violent ways to get their message across – such as sending letter bombs.

At the other end of the spectrum, many people support human rights over the rights of animals. These campaigners tend to join forces over specific issues. Many of the 20 million people who watch bullfights every year consider this an important tradition and sport. Hunters argue that animal numbers need to be controlled, or that shooting provides valuable income. Sometimes animals come second simply because people consider human life to be more valuable, for example in medical experiments.

Economics of animal welfare

Conditions or provisions that improve welfare often come at a high price. Farming is an excellent example of the relationship between animal welfare and economics. **Intensive farming** may seem the ideal way to produce animals cheaply and profitably. Many animals can be raised on a small land area, and food and labour requirements are lower than on extensive farms. The profit per animal is small, since supermarkets pay less for intensively reared meat, but the vast number of animals that can be produced compensates for this. In dairy farms, for example, herd sizes and animal milk yields in some countries have more than doubled since 1975. Although these mass production systems are efficient, some of the conditions associated with them can be at the cost of animal well-being.

Free-range farming, usually offering higher levels of animal welfare, costs more since it requires larger land areas, more food and more staff. To the public, free-range foods represent quality and so the products command a higher price. Supermarkets pay the farmer more – and pass this price on to the consumer. With this premium price a free-range farmer can in theory make a similar profit to an intensive farmer, with fewer animals.

Many farmers are sympathetic to the well-being of their stock, but the expense of converting to a profitable free-range system is often prohibitive. Productive land is an expensive commodity in the industrialized world. Coupled with the demolition of intensive buildings and construction of new barns, this is a high price to pay. During the conversion period, the farmer stands to make little profit on the empty farm, and may require new breeds when able to restock. Animal welfare improvements are often blocked by the cost. However, many Western governments, especially in Northern Europe, are encouraging farmers to

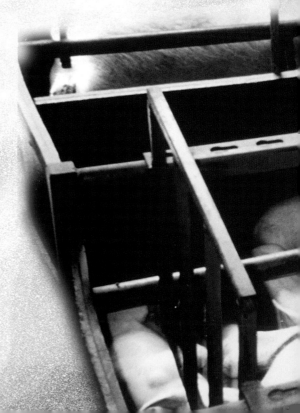

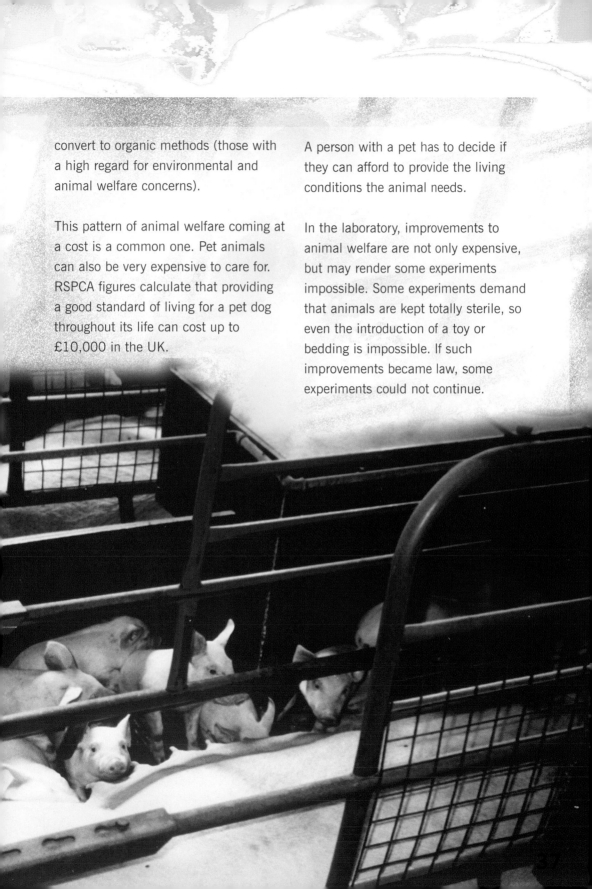

convert to organic methods (those with a high regard for environmental and animal welfare concerns).

This pattern of animal welfare coming at a cost is a common one. Pet animals can also be very expensive to care for. RSPCA figures calculate that providing a good standard of living for a pet dog throughout its life can cost up to £10,000 in the UK.

A person with a pet has to decide if they can afford to provide the living conditions the animal needs.

In the laboratory, improvements to animal welfare are not only expensive, but may render some experiments impossible. Some experiments demand that animals are kept totally sterile, so even the introduction of a toy or bedding is impossible. If such improvements became law, some experiments could not continue.

Developing countries

Developing countries face different animal welfare problems. These countries are also reliant on agriculture, whether for local use from smallholdings, or cash crops grown in bulk for the international market. Animals also feature in other parts of the economy. In some countries wild animals may be caught for sale as food – known as bush meat – into the pet trade or to research laboratories. Other animals such as bears are trained to dance, whilst baby animals attract tourists who will pay to be photographed with them.

In the developing world, famine, drought and starvation are common. Countries struggle to support rapidly growing human populations and there are few, if any, animal protection laws. Many animals are being hunted near to extinction so that people may survive.

All available productive land is required to feed growing populations. Where land is poor or desertified, interest is growing in **intensive farms**. These farms are expensive to set up, however, and so the majority of farms are still run in a traditional way, with animals herded or tethered.

Bush meat kill in the Congo: wild monkey and antelopes.

Tortoise trading

Tortoises are one of the most popular animals in the exotic pet trade. More than 25 species are legally protected, and yet illegal trade continues to increase. In 2001, undercover investigation revealed rare tortoises openly for sale at markets in Morocco. Tortoise sellers assured the investigators that these animals could be imported to another country in a box or bag and were easy to care for.

In developing countries, where the economy may be unsteady, animal trade is one of only a few sources of income. Animals like the tortoise are easily caught and packed up. In one illegal shipment opened by Dutch customs officials, 800 tortoises were packed in layers in a box. 50 were dead and 400 more in a critical condition. A large number had broken shells and missing legs. Had this cargo not been discovered and confiscated, the animals would have raised a substantial profit.

In recent years, developing countries have benefited from the strict animal welfare regulations in developed countries. When cosmetic testing on animals is banned in one country, laboratories simply move elsewhere. This is often to the cheap land and labour of developing countries, where new infrastructures and employment are vitally needed.

Animal welfare laws

Countries vary in the level of protection that they offer to animals. This reflects the economic climate as much as the value placed on animals. A wealthy country can afford high standards. For a country facing famine and human suffering, relieving that of animals may not be such a priority. Examples of animal protection laws are given below.

New Zealand

The most recent form of animal protection is the Animal Welfare Act 1999. This law extends to all animals. It is considered an offence to knowingly cause an animal to become disabled, die or have to be destroyed following ill treatment. A person can be imprisoned for up to three years or fined $50,000.

Australia

In Australia, each State and Territory has a Prevention of Cruelty to Animals Act. This controls all uses of animals including animal experimentation, except in New South Wales, which has a separate Act. The **legislation** does not define cruelty but lists actions and inactions that are thought to be acts of cruelty.

The USA

Each State has its own animal protection laws. In 33 States animal abuse is classed as a felony rather than a misdemeanour.

Puppies in overcrowded cages, Indiana, USA. The American Kennel Club is lobbying against legislation that would specify conditions for dog-breeding.

The UK

In the UK, the Protection of Animals Act 1911 still operates but has been added to and improved ever since. The basic principles of the Act are:

- It is against the law cruelly to overload, beat, kick, ill-treat, torture or terrify an animal.
- It is against the law to make an animal suffer when it does not have to.
- It is against the law to abandon an animal if it will suffer when it does not have to.

European Law

Throughout Europe different countries have individual animal protection laws. Increasingly, however, the European Parliament is demanding that laws become standardized across the European Union, to bring members to the same level of animal protection in law.

Increased concerns over animal welfare are continually being reflected in new laws. For example, in 2001 the Humane Methods of Slaughter Act was passed by the US Senate. Although existing Acts from 1958 and 1978 were in place, these were not consistently upheld. This new Act states that all animals must be rendered insensible to pain before death, and that the Department of Agriculture must track any violations that occur.

International co-operation

The Convention on International Trade in **Endangered** Species of Wild Flora and Fauna (CITES) recommendations to control the trade in endangered species came into effect in 1975. To date, 146 nations including the USA, Australia and the UK have signed up to this agreement. The main purpose of the agreement is to prevent animals becoming extinct, but it can affect individual welfare too.

The countries in agreement with CITES prohibit commercial trade in endangered species. Now the animal trade has turned to smuggling to meet the demand for rare animals. The trade is second only to drug smuggling in its illegal moneymaking potential – at least £4 billion a year.

Despite CITES animal smuggling is hard to control since exotic and rare species are highly desirable. People can often earn much-needed money from the capture and sale of creatures they have traditionally hunted for food and skins. Sometimes countries argue that the animals will be used for valuable research or breeding. No one can deny though, that animals suffer enormously during this process. Around 75 per cent of captured wild animals die in transit. Nine out of ten survivors will die in the following four years.

This trade is hard to detect and control. Some countries invest more than others in trying to prevent illegal trade. In Australia, for example, wildlife trade law is the most advanced in the world. The new Environment Protection and Biodiversity Amendment (Wildlife Protection) **Bill** 2001 sets best practice standards for the world, increasing the ease with which the Federal Government can **prosecute** offenders.

The world's most wanted bird

The deep, brilliant blue Lear's macaw comes from north-east Brazil. Up until 1978 these birds were thought to be extinct. Only 98 Lear's macaws are known to exist. As a result they are the most wanted birds in the world, worth £80,000 each.

In 1988 three Lear's macaws were found in a house in Yorkshire, England. They had been smuggled into the country, perhaps inside other cargo. Poster tubes are often used in smuggling, with a bird crammed headfirst into each end of the tube. Before they even arrive, over 75 per cent will be dead. Parrots often peck each other or themselves to death on their journey.

Hyacinth macaws.

Campaigning for change

Around the world, animal laws show a great deal of variation. Laws are constantly being amended and updated, usually to introduce higher levels of protection for animals.

Many organizations involved in areas of the animal industry draw up their own codes of practice to ensure good standards. Frequently these codes become incorporated into law itself. Animal welfare organizations often investigate 'best practice' and will attempt to get this recognized in **legislation**.

Changes to animal welfare legislation come about when an issue is brought to the attention of the public and the government. Many governments have advisory bodies to oversee areas of potential concern. The European Parliament is guided by the Standing Veterinary Committee and the Scientific Committee on Animal Health and Animal Welfare. Animal welfare organizations that are not connected to the government, often charities supported by public funds, may also be called on for their expertise.

In some instances, both multinational organizations that use animals and pressure groups from animal welfare organizations will lobby governments to support their interests. Companies with the finances to advertise the ways they have used animals for human benefit put forward a powerful argument.

Activists demonstrating against a bull fight in Montreal, Canada, 1999.

Animal welfare organizations, often reliant on public support and donations, have to be increasingly sophisticated and scientific if they are to make their case. The group that has the most effective campaign may well push its own viewpoint to the forefront.

The process of lobbying includes researching and preparing evidence, statistics and reports. The more the media is involved and publicity raised, the greater the chance of success in gaining the attention of the government. If the campaign is successful, new laws can be brought in, or old ones amended and reformed.

Before most elected officials will introduce animal-friendly legislation, they must be convinced that there is sufficient public support. When the state of Virginia in the USA was considering bringing in a bounty on coyotes the governor received so much mail against the bounty that he dropped the bill. The Governor of New York, Mario Cuomo, twice rejected a bill that would have allowed medical technicians to practise fitting human breathing tubes on cats. The Governor's office received more mail about this than any other piece of legislation.

Animal rights activists dressed as chickens protest against battery cages, outside a meeting of European Union farm ministers in Brussels, 1999.

Animal welfare and you

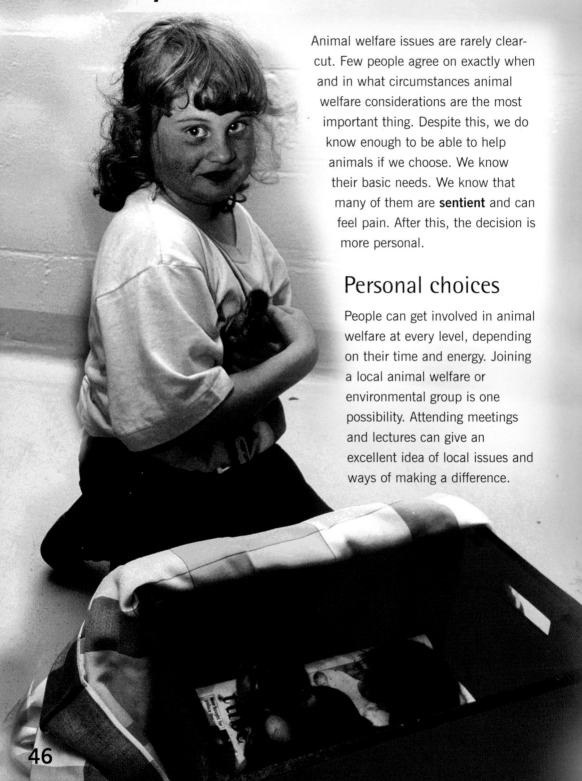

Animal welfare issues are rarely clear-cut. Few people agree on exactly when and in what circumstances animal welfare considerations are the most important thing. Despite this, we do know enough to be able to help animals if we choose. We know their basic needs. We know that many of them are **sentient** and can feel pain. After this, the decision is more personal.

Personal choices

People can get involved in animal welfare at every level, depending on their time and energy. Joining a local animal welfare or environmental group is one possibility. Attending meetings and lectures can give an excellent idea of local issues and ways of making a difference.

Some groups get involved in writing awareness-raising letters to government, giving you the chance to have a say in national politics.

Many animal shelters and clinics offer work experience or weekend work. Animal centres often rely on volunteers, as their own funds may be limited. Volunteers may clean pens or walk dogs, helping improve animals' lives and gaining valuable work experience at the same time.

Actions that we take in our every day lives can directly influence animal welfare. The following suggestions are things you can do to help.

• If you see an act of cruelty, contact your local SPCA or equivalent. Do not try to intervene – think of your own welfare first.

• If you have a pet make sure you know how to care for it properly.

• Buy cruelty-free products where possible. Failing that, avoid 'new' products – a new type of washing powder, for example, will have

been developed with many more animal tests. Eco-friendly products are less polluting, which is beneficial to the health and welfare of animals and the environment.

• Disposing of rubbish carefully can prevent accidental injury to wild animals.

• Shopping for **free-range** products promotes non-**intensive farming** and its associated standards of animal welfare. Going one step further might be becoming vegetarian or vegan, and not eating or using animal products at all. The less meat is consumed overall, the less intensive production is needed.

• Avoid using garden chemicals and instead encourage predatory wildlife such as ladybirds to control unwanted insects. If you dig a pond, put up a bird table, plant wild flowers and recycle your organic waste in a compost heap, your garden is well on the way to being animal friendly.

What next?

Issues surrounding animal welfare can be complex. Research continually teaches us more, and yet there are no easy rights or wrongs. When human and animal interests are in competition people support a whole range of opinions, according to their experience, knowledge, religion and situation.

When people buy food, medicines and clothes, they are involved in the animal debate. Consumers can often choose products that are more – or less – animal friendly. If they can afford to, they have the choice of buying **free range** rather than **intensively** reared meat. They can decide whether to wear fur or not. Leisure time can be spent fishing, hunting or walking. Buying power can create new markets – whether they involve more or less animal welfare.

At the zoo, debate centres on keeping animals in captivity. There is proof that animals suffer in many zoos, but conditions can be improved. Zoos also claim a role in the breeding and re-introduction of **endangered** species that would otherwise be lost.

Around the world there are billions of pets. Some of these have been caught illegally in the wild and transported to pet shops thousands of miles away. Puppies may be reared for sale on vast puppy farms, or they can come from small litters and breeders who care for their dogs.

> **❝When I carefully consider**
> the curious habits
> of dogs
> I am compelled to conclude
> That man is the superior animal.
>
> When I consider the curious habits
> of man
> I confess, my friend,
> I am puzzled.❞
>
> (Ezra Pound, poet (1885–1972))

The debate over animals used for scientific research is heated. Many researchers rely on animals as models for people. Animals are used in tests for cosmetics, weapons and new treatments for diseases like AIDS. There is opposition to this research and the suffering it causes to animals, and so work continues to find suitable alternatives.

Animal welfare is a personal issue. People choose how to lead their lives, and directly and indirectly these choices can impact on animal welfare.

Facts and figures

These figures are just a snapshot of what is going on in the world where animals are involved. For each group of animals covered there is an example and some general figures for animal use, ownership and treatment.

Farming

Around 100,000 horses a year are involved in the production of **Hormone Replacement Therapies**. Pregnant mares are kept in small stalls for six months so that their urine can be collected. After birth the mare's foal is usually destroyed so that she can quickly get pregnant again.

The average Briton eats 550 chickens, 36 pigs, 36 sheep, eight cattle and dairy products equivalent to 18 tonnes of milk in their life.

In 1996, 760 million chickens were reared for meat in the UK. Of these, more than 45 million died early from illness and genetic defects.

Australia exports 5 million sheep to the Middle East each year.

Research

In addition to commercial animal tests, around US$200 million a year is spent by the US Department of Defense on animal research. This involves around 1.6 million animals. Examples of the research programmes include: shooting 700 cats to model human injuries; developing surgical techniques on pigs; testing poison gases on rats and mice. UK Home Office Statistics for 2000 show that 2.71 million experimental procedures were carried out on animals. 500,000 of these animals were **genetically modified** – a 14 per cent increase on 1999. In Australia, 3 million animals were used in scientific research in 1998

Companion animals

The RSPCA rescued a badly neglected Monitor lizard from a house whose owner had moved. The lizard had an infection so severe it could no longer move, and was **put down** to end its suffering.

In 2000 RSPCA Australia shelters cared for 138,670 animals. In the same year there were 47,000 cruelty investigations.

In the USA, 13 million unwanted pets are destroyed each year.

Wildlife

The killer whale (orca) was first taken in to captivity in 1961. Since then 134 others have been put in **aquaria**. In the wild they live over 50 years and swim more than 150 kilometres a day. In captivity 78 per cent have so far died, most before six years old.

In the USA 200 million animals are hunted each year; 3.5 million are trapped for fur.

In China and Korea 7500 bears are kept caged, and their bile is collected for medicine.

Sources:
IFAW; RSPCA, ASPCA, WWF, WSPA, RDS, UK Government Home Office Statistics

Performing killer whale, Aqualand, California.

Further information

Contacts in the UK

Animal Aid
The Old Chapel, Bradford Street, Tonbridge,
Kent TN9 1AW Tel: 01732 364 546
email: info@animalaid.org.ok
www.animalaid.org.uk

Blue Cross
Shilton Road,Burford, Oxon OX18 4PF
Tel: 01993 825500
email: sarahm@bluecross.org.uk
www.bluecross.org.uk

Compassion in World Farming
Charles House, 5a Charles Street,
Petersfield, Hants Tel: 01730 264208
email: compassion@ciwf.co.uk
www.ciwf.co.uk

Fight Against Animal Cruelty in Europe
29 Shakespeare Street,
Southport, Merseyside PR8 5AB
Tel: 01704 535922
email: action@faace.co.uk
www.faace.co.uk

**Fund for the Replacement of Animals in
Medical Experiments**
96–98 North Sherwood House,
Nottingham, NG1 4EE Tel: 0115 958 4740
email: frame@frame.org.uk
www.frame.org.uk

Research Defence Society
58 Great Marlborough Street,
London W1F 7JY Tel: 020 7287 288
email: info@rds-online.org.uk
www.rds-online.org.uk

RSPCA
Wilberforce Way, Southwater,
Horsham, West Sussex RH13 9RS
Tel: 0870 0101 181
email: enquiries@rspca.org.uk
www.rspca.org.uk

Seriously Ill for Medical Research
PO Box 504, Dunstable,
Bedfordshire LU6 2LU Tel: 01582 873108
email: andrew.blake@simr.org.uk
www.simr.org.uk

The Vegan Society
Donald Watson House, 7 Battle Road,
St Leonards on Sea, East Sussex TN37 7AA
Tel: 01424 427393
email: info@vegansociety.com
www.vegansociety.com

The Vegetarian Society
Parkdale, Dunham Road, Altrincham,
Cheshire WA14 4QG Tel: 0161 925 2000
email: info@vegsoc.org
www.vegsoc.org

**World Society for the Protection of Animals
(WSPA)**
89 Albert Embankment, London SE1 7TP
Tel: 020 7587 5000
email: wspa@wspa.org.uk
www.wspa.org.uk

World Wide Fund for Nature (WWF)
Panda House, Weyside Park, Godalming,
Surrey GU7 1XR Tel: 01483 426444
www.panda.org

Contacts in the USA

American Anti Vivisection Society
801 Old York Rd #204
Jenkintown, PA 19046-1685
email: aavsonline@aol.com
www.aavs.org

American SPCA
424E 92nd Street, New York, NY 10128
www.aspca.org

American Humane Association
63 Inverness Drive East,
Englewood, CO 80112-5117

email: info@amercianhumane.org
www.americanhumane.org

Americans for Medical Progress
908 King Street, Suite 201,
Alexandria, VA 22314
email: info@amprogress.org
www.ampef.org

The Humane Society of the United States
200 L Street NW, Washington D.C. 20037
email: webmaster@hsus.org
www.hsus.org

International Fund for Animal Welfare
International HQ, 411 Main Street,
PO Box 193, Yarmouth Port, MA 02675
email: info@ifaw.org
www.ifaw.org

National Association for Biomedical Research
818 Conneticut Avenue NW,
Suite 200, Washington D.C. 20006
Tel: (1) 202 857 0540 email: info@nabr.org
www.nabr.org

People for the Ethical Treatment of Animals
501 Front Street, Norfolk, VA 23510
Tel: (1) 767 622 7385
email: info@peta-online.org
www.peta-online.org

Contacts in Australia

Animal Rights Resource Centre
PO Box 18, Kent Town, S. Australia 5071
Tel: (61) 08 8351 1615
info@arrc.org.au
www.arrc.org.au

RSPCA Australia
RSPCA Australia Inc., PO Box 265,
Deakin West, ACT 2600, Australia
Tel: (61) 2 6282 8300
email: rspca@rspca.org.au
www.rspca.org.au

Contacts in New Zealand

New Zealand Anti Vivisection Society
PO Box 9387, Christchurch, New Zealand
email: Phil@kiwimail.net.nz
www.nzavs.org.nz

Royal New Zealand SPCA
PO Box 15349, New Lynn,
Auckland 7, New Zealand
Tel: (64) 09 827 6094
email: info@rnzspca.org.nz
www.rspcanz.org.nz

Further reading

Animals Behind Bars, Sylvia Funston
(Scholastic Ltd, 1999)

The Young Person's Action Guide to Animal Rights, Barbara James (Virago Press Ltd, 1992)

Born to be Wild, Juliet Gellatley (Livewire Books, 2000)

Animal Welfare, Colin Spedding (Earthscan Publications Ltd, 2000)

Glossary

anthropomorphism
giving human form or feelings to an animal or object

aquarium/aquaria
tanks or buildings containing water animals and plants

Bill
draft of an Act of Parliament

bull baiting
sport in which bulldogs are pitted against restrained bulls

Caesarean section
delivery of offspring by cutting into the mother's abdomen

captive bolt
bolt shot into the brain to stun an animal

cholera
bacterial infection causing diarrhoea

clone
animal produced artificially from the cells of one parent. It is identical to the parent and has the same genes.

compassion
feeling of pity or distress at another's suffering

coral
marine animal that lives in large communities and builds an often stony skeleton

cortisones
chemical hormones made in the body which carry signals through the blood to another part of the body

DNA
molecule found in the cells of an organism. It contains all the information needed to build and maintain the organism.

domesticate
to keep wildlife under control or cultivation

embalmed
treated with preservatives to stop decay

endangered
facing extinction (dying out)

endorphins
chemicals made in the body which carry a painkilling signal through the blood to another part of the body

exploitation
using for one's own gain

free range
farming system where animals have room to move around and access to the outdoors

gene
length of DNA that describes one characteristic of an organism – e.g. eye colour

genetic engineering
field of science in which genes are moved or altered to make changes to organisms

genetic modification
the process of altering the DNA in an organism

habitat
natural home of an animal or plant

hormone
chemical made by the body

Hormone Replacement Therapy
treatment for women during and after the menopause

intensive farming
farming for maximum production, usually highly mechanized; animals are often kept indoors

legislation
laws or the process of making laws

moratorium
agreed suspension of activity

neurological
of the nervous system or brain

prosecution
carrying out legal proceedings against someone

put down
kill humanely, usually by injection

quarry
intended prey

selective breeding
deliberate breeding of animals to improve certain characteristics

sentience
the state of being sentient – see below

sentient
having the power of sense perception or sensation

snaring
trapping animals with a wire loop that catches hold and draws in tighter

sow
female adult pig

stereotypy/stereotypies
repetitive movement – such as pacing, rocking or foot chewing – as a reaction to stress

transgenic
containing genetic material artificially moved from other organisms

vivisection
experimentation on living animals

weaned
taken off milk and started on solid food

Index